Picture credits:
t=top b=bottom c=centre l=left r=right m=middle

Front Cover Images: fleag/istock: c, Sean Nel/Shutterstock: b, Michael Fuery/Shutterstock: mb, Rafa Irusta/Shutterstock: cr, Stephen Finn/Shutterstock: bl, Trutta55/Shutterstock: t, Mikulich Alexander Andreevich/shutterstock: br, IlyaGenkin/Shutterstock: ml, Bukvarj/Shutterstock: mb,

Back Cover Images: javarman/shutterstock: t, Eric Gevaert/shutterstock: c, Eric Gevaert/Shutterstock: m,

Border Images: Michael Fuery/Shutterstock, kwest/Shutterstock, Terrance Emerson/Shutterstock, Rafa Irusta/Shutterstock, Trutta55/Shutterstock, Juan Fuertes/Shutterstock,

Insides: Andrejs Zemdega/iStockphoto: 6tl, Elshaneo/Dreamstime: 6-7b, Jason Scott Duggan/Shutterstock: 8br, Bob Hosea/Shutterstock: 9, Henk Bentlage/Shutterstock: 10-11, Stacey Newman/iStockphoto: 11br, M.i.k.e/Shutterstock: 12-13, Brenda Arlene Smith/iStockphoto: 12br, Razvan/istock: 13tr, Island Effects/istock: 14b, WizData, inc./Shutterstock: 14-15r, Simon Gurney/iStockphoto:15br, Sherry Sowell/iStockphoto: 18tl, Socrates/Shutterstock: 18-19, Alistair Scott/Shutterstock: 19mr, Richard Huston/fotolia: 20ml, Rainer/Dreamstime: 20-21 Dgilder/Dreamstime: 21tr, Ralph125/ iStockphoto: 22tl, Fabio Bianchini/iStockphoto: 22blPetr Nad/Shutterstock: 22-23, Eric Cabasse/ fotolia: 24t, Solar cooking.org: 24tr, Shi Yali/Shutterstock: 24-25b, Donald R. Swartz/Shutterstock: 26tl, Mark Jensen/iStockphoto: 26-27b, alafia/flickr: 27tr, Elena Elisseeva/shutterstock: 28-29, Kyle Smith/Shutterstock: 29br, Aloha/istock: 30tl, Jeancliclac/fotolia: 31tr, Mona Makela/Shutterstock: 30-31, Massimiliano Lamagna/Shutterstock: 33tr, Spion Kop/Flickr: 32mr, Ron Mcqueeney: 32cb, Pryzmat/Dreamstime: 34m, Starfotograf/istock: 35tl, Alexey Stiop/shutterstock: 35mr, Kathy Burns-Millyard/shutterstock: 36-37ct, Slawomir Kruz/Shutterstock: 36ml, Ronen/shutterstock: 37br, Johanna Goodyear/Shutterstock: 38-39ctr, Rohit Seth/Shutterstock: 38ml, JynMeyerDesign/istock: 38ml, Rafael Laguillo/Dreamstime: 39mr, Joe Gough/Shutterstock: 42-43cm, Joe Gough/Shutterstock: 42ml, Stacy Barnett/Dreamstime: 43tr.

ALL ILLUSTRATIONS MADE BY Q2A MEDIA

Published By: Robert Frederick Ltd.
4 North Parade, Bath, BA1 1LF, UK

First Published: 2008

HYDROGEN & VEGGIE OIL POWERED

Green Revolution

CONTENTS

World Today

Our earth has been around for billions of years. However, in the past 150 years, human activity has led to faster changes than the world has seen in thousands of years.

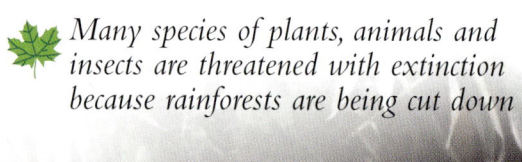
Trees are being cut down to make space for people to live and work

Many species of plants, animals and insects are threatened with extinction because rainforests are being cut down

Trees, Please!

Land makes up only a third of the earth's surface. Until a few hundred years ago, much of this land was covered with forest. In a forest, the trees are so close together that their crowns touch and look like one large canopy. But these forests have steadily been cut down for wood and to make more land available for roads, factories and towns.

Where's My Home?

Trees and forests are home to a vast variety of wildlife. If the rainforests were to disappear, almost half the world's plants, animals and insects would lose their home. In order to run factories and produce more electricity, huge amounts of coal, oil, iron-ore and other natural resources are being mined from inside the earth. These are resources that take millions of years to form and we are losing them faster than the earth can make them.

Phew, it's Hot!

Plants make food by taking in carbon dioxide - a gas that is harmful to us and causes global warming - and giving out oxygen. However, in the last hundred years or so, emissions from factories and vehicles, have been releasing more and more harmful gases, such as carbon dioxide. Cutting down trees disturbs the balance between oxygen and carbon dioxide in the air.

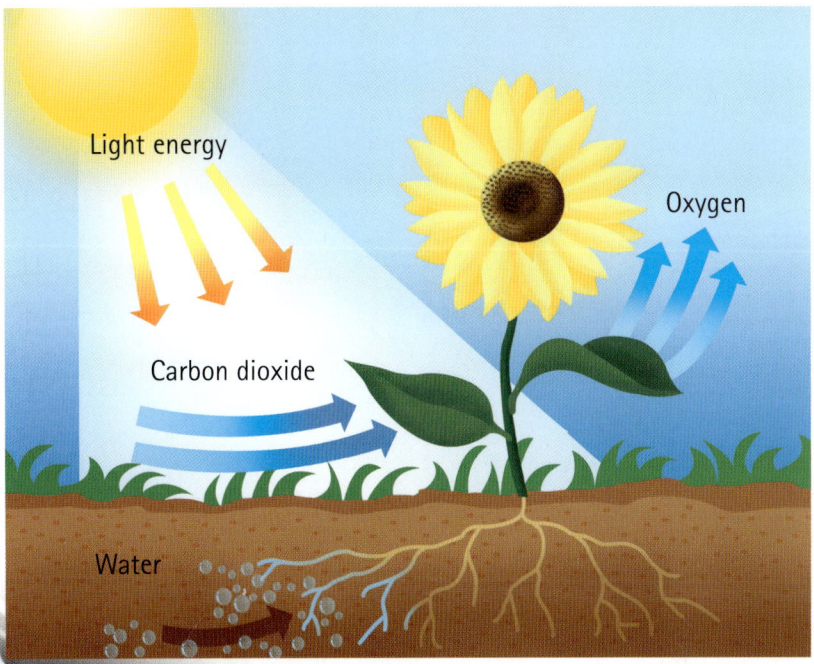

Light energy

Oxygen

Carbon dioxide

Water

Plants make their food with the help of sunlight, carbon dioxide and water. This is known as photosynthesis

ECO fact

Many medicines prescribed by doctors are made from plants. Approximately one in four medicines is made using ingredients from rainforest trees.

Deforestation

Cutting down forests in order to make space available for farming and other purposes is known as deforestation. This has knock-on effects for the environment.

Machines More Than People

The Industrial Revolution introduced new machines that required fuel, rather than manpower, to operate. These machines worked better and faster and produced goods that could be sold to new markets, home and abroad. New factory towns sprang up where earlier there were forests. Forests are being destroyed even today to make way for more roads and towns.

Looms were introduced during the Industrial Revolution to weave yarn into textiles

Wood is Good but Trees are Better

Forests are being cut down to make way for more roads, railway lines and airports. They are also being cut down for wood in order to make furniture, doors, windows, etc. Around 3 million people in developing countries all over the world rely on wood for cooking and other purposes. Moreover, factories need more oil and ores, which have to be mined from the ground. This also leads to forests being cut down. The discovery of gold at Seven Mile Diggings in Australia set off a flood of people settling in the region from the late 19th century. Large areas covered with forests were cleared to accomodate the new settlers.

Forests are cut down to make way for digging deep underground mines

Chop, Chop, Chop

Factories and industries are growing rapidly all over the world. Better railways and shipping routes have helped industries in different parts of the world to share resources. Countries like China, where most people worked in fields until only about 20 years ago, are now producing almost everything, from dolls to computers. To keep these industries going, the factories need oil. They are clearing forests in order to make roads and railways, so that they can reach oil reserves in countries as far away as Rwanda and Nigeria, in Africa.

In Peru, South America, 127,700 hectares of dense rainforests had been cleared each year between 1999 and 2005!

ECO fact

About 6,000 acres of rainforest are being chopped down every hour.

Grave Impact

Forests are important for the evolution of life on earth. They support a level of biodiversity not found anywhere else in the world.

Home, Sweet Home

Forests are home to more than half of all the species of animals on earth. When trees are cut down they are left homeless. The World Conservation Union, or IUCN, found that one in three species of apes, monkeys and other primates are faced with extinction. This is mainly due to habitat destruction, sale of their meat and skin and illegal trade in wildlife. Some primates are also taken away from their natural habitats to be kept as pets and for entertainment.

Gorillas, orangutans and lemurs are among the world's 25 most endangered primate species

ECO fact

The earth is getting warmer. The temperature of the earth's surface rose 0.74 C (1.33 F) between 1905 and 2005.

Soaking Up The Poison

Greenhouse gases, such as carbon dioxide and methane, trap heat in the earth's atmosphere. An excess of greenhouse gases is harmful for life on earth. Trees play an important part in maintaining the carbon balance in air. Cutting down trees is increasing its amount in the atmosphere and contributing to global warming.

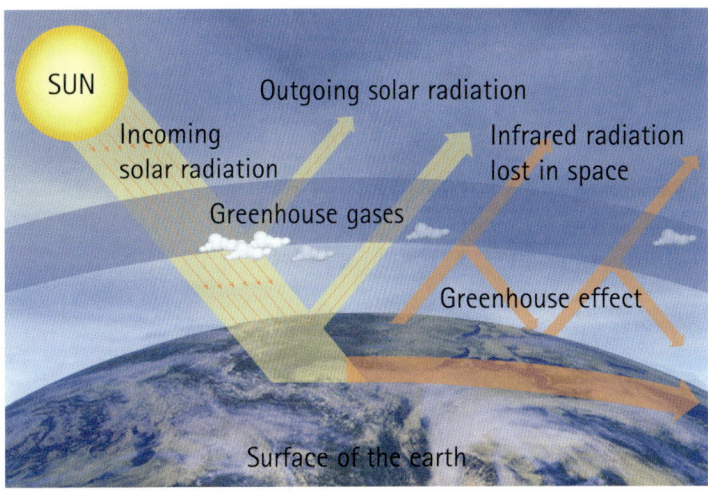

Incoming solar radiation is absorbed and re-emitted by greenhouse gas molecules, causing global warming

Drying Up

Trees play an important role in water balance. Their roots draw water from the ground, which the leaves release into the air through transpiration. With forests being cut down, this balance is being destroyed. This is especially true of places with broad-leaved trees, such as the tropical rainforests.

Water could soon grow scarce in the Amazon basin

Turning Green

Forests need not be lost forever. There are ways in which they can be preserved to redress the ecological balance in the world. Afforestation and reforestation are two ways to conserve and grow new forests.

Afforestation and Reforestation

Trees can be grown from seeds and forests can be regrown by planting young trees in spaces that have not been forested for a period of time. Afforestation includes agricultural lands and pastures for which forests had been cut down a long time ago. Reforestation means regrowing forests on lands that had forests but were damaged due to forest fire, disease, pests, drought or other natural causes. Places are afforested and reforested to decrease the level of environmental damage.

Each of us can make a small difference by planting a tree

Going Official

The problem of deforestation was noted in the Kyoto Protocol. The protocol came into effect on February 16, 2005. It was an international agreement on climate change, held to find ways to reduce the impact of greenhouse gases and global warming. One of the recommendations of the the Kyoto Protocol was to encouraged afforestation and reforestation on land that had been cleared or poorly forested, in order to fight the problem of global warming.

The Kyoto Protocol was formulated in Japan. Delegates came from all over the world to discuss the problem of global warming

Turn Local

It is important to plant trees that are local to a region, especially when a forest is being re-planted. Native trees have an advantage over trees that are naturally found in other climatic zones. They often grow better where they are meant to be and need little extra care. They are also less likely to be attacked by germs and harmful insects. Sometimes, plants and trees brought from outside can grow so fast that they take away space from the native species. This affects local insects, birds, and animals as well because they often cannot find food. Alien plants also increase the instances of disease in trees.

Many trees and forests are destroyed by raging forest fires. Reforestation is one way to make sure that we can regrow trees in areas where they've been lost

ECO fact

Since 1990, the European Union pays farmers who turn farmlands into forests. Europe has more forests today than a hundred years ago, due to afforestation.

Big Help

Trees help us in many ways and their benefits extend far beyond their impact on climate.

Hold the Soil

Tree roots hold the soil together and protect it from being washed away by heavy rain. The topsoil is extremely precious, as it takes between 100-500 years for an inch to form, depending on the climate and type of rock. When this soil is washed away, it settles in riverbeds and lakes as silt. This reduces the amount of water these rivers can hold and also causes floods. In the hills, roots of trees prevent the soil and rocks from slipping downhill as landslides.

Leaves of trees form an umbrella over the land and break the force of rain water that can wash away soil

ECO fact

Trees help keep us happy and fit. Hockey sticks, cricket and baseball bats, and tennis racquets are all made of wood.

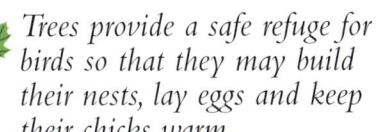
Trees provide a safe refuge for birds so that they may build their nests, lay eggs and keep their chicks warm

Natural Coolers

Trees absorb carbon dioxide, keeping the air cool and clean. Leaves clean the air by absorbing dust and other harmful particles. During the day, they release oxygen, which we breathe. They also release water vapour into the air. These droplets of vapour form clouds and bring us rain. Trees are a natural home for millions of animals, birds and insects. They also help to break the speed of wind. This stops the spread of deserts (desertification).

Other Uses

Trees have many other uses and their parts are used in different ways. Medicines are made from their bark, leaves, fruit, flowers and roots. Tree houses are home to people who live in forests. Many products, such as cosmetics, are also made from trees.

Wooden tree houses fascinate and provide adventure to both children and adults

15

Thousands of women from villages came out in protest during the famous Chipko Movement

The Drive for Green

Saving and protecting trees ensures a better and healthier environment for people to live in.

The Chipko Movement

The Chipko Movement was an inspiring event related to the Green Revolution. The Hindi word *Chipko* means, 'to stick'. In 1973, a group of women in the Chamoli region of north India hugged trees to prevent them from being cut down by the government forest department. Some men also joined them in their protest and soon the Chipko Movement spread throughout the region.

The Khejarli Story

Khejarli is a village in the northern part of India. The village got its name from the Khejri tree that grows there. In 1730, several residents of the village gave their lives in order to protect the Khejri trees from being cut down by the king's men. The movement was started by Amrita Devi, a lady belonging to the Bishnoi sect, which held all life sacred and opposed the cutting down of trees and killing of animals.

Richard St. Barbe Baker is widely known as The Man of the Trees. In 1979, the Prince of Wales became the Patron of his organisation

363 people died saving the Khejri trees in the Khejarli village

Going Green

Richard St. Barbe Baker (1889-1982) was an English environmental activist who served in Kenya as the Assistant Conservator of Forests. In 1922, he joined hands with the Kenyans and approached the tribesmen to help in tree planting. Almost 3000 people came forward to help him in this venture. He formed a committee with 50 of these men and called them *Watu wa Miti*, or Men of the Trees. This organisation later grew in size and spread to many other countries.

More To Do

The Green Revolution is an ongoing change in the process of agriculture, which began in the 1940s. The movement led to an increase in the level of food production needed to keep pace with the rising population levels around the world.

High-yielding varieties of seeds, such as cotton, produce more crops

The Green Revolution encouraged production of more crops with the help of better farm machines and fertilisers

Growing Green

In 1968, William Gaud, the director of USAID, looked at the sudden improvements in agriculture and called it the Green Revolution. It was a planned international effort and was financed by international organisations, such as the Rockefeller Foundation, Ford Foundation and the governments of several developing countries. This change was possible because of improved technology and research in agriculture. Chemical fertilisers and pesticides, better farm machinery and high yielding varieties of seeds were used together to improve crops.

Negative Impact

The Green Revolution had some negative impacts as well. It encouraged people to grow crops that would be most productive. This meant most farmers changed from multi-cropping to cultivating one crop that produced more yield. The new techniques also resulted in growing crops that were meant for export and not for daily consumption. As a result, even with increased crop production, farmers were not able to live off the food produced on their farms and had to look for other sources of food. The increased production also needed fertilisers and pesticides, which changed the make-up of the soil, making them less fertile.

Green Turns Red

The use of fertilisers and pesticides and artificial means to grow crops, changed the quality of the soil. Some fields ended up having too much salt and others too little. In some places, the soil became alkaline. It also brought in poisons, such as arsenic, and led to a drop in the water table in some regions. The Rio Treaty (1992) acknowledged the negative effects of the movement and 189 nations signed the treaty to take Biodiversity Action Plans to counter the negative effect.

 The over use of chemical pesticides ruined the quality of soil in many places

ECO fact

Norman Earnest Bolaug won the Nobel Peace Prize in 1970 for his work on wheat breeding.

Organic Advantages

Chemical fertilisers were first used in the 19th century. However, when their harmful effects became obvious, the organic movement started.

What Is Organic Farming?

Organic farming only uses natural fertilisers, such as manure, and natural pesticides. No chemical fertilisers or pesticides are used. Moreover, instead of growing just one crop, organic farmers rotate crops, growing different plants on one farm, to discourage pests and loss of the nutrient value of the soil. Food that has been grown according to the methods laid down by the International Federation of Organic Agriculture Movements carries the organic label.

Back To The Roots

The Green Revolution introduced monoculture, or growing only one kind of crop for higher yield. As a result many types of seeds were lost. But, during the organic movement, new seed banks were set up to collect wild and local seeds. Traditional ways of growing crops were also slowly re-introduced. Farmers in some places returned to organic farming, using natural fertilisers and pesticides.

The organic movement has made organic foods increasingly popular

The organic movement encourages the use of traditional and natural fertilisers, such as manure

Eat Organic

We can take in tiny amounts of pesticides when we eat crops that have been sprayed. Pesticide residues are found in all kinds of food, from fruit to milk and even baby food. But organic farms do not use chemical fertilisers. Animals brought up on an organic farm are not fed growth hormones to grow faster. Organic foods are rich in vitamins and minerals. They are considered by many to taste better too. However, organic food does come at a premium in price.

Arround 310,000 square kilometres (75 million acres) of land is under organic farming

ECO fact

The United Kingdom uses about 31,000 tonnes (34,171 tons) of pesticides every year.

Alternative Energy

The demand for energy is growing. The constant increase in population is leading to the use of more cars and electricity. The constant use of different sources of energy leads to more pollution and the fear of its depletion.

Vehicles are one of the largest sources of hazardous air pollutants or HAPs

What Most of us Use

Most vehicles run on fossil fuels. These include coal, petroleum and natural gas. These fuels take millions of years to form. Continuous and extensive use of such fossil fuels will eventually lead to their depletion. Fossil fuels also cause a lot of pollution. They lead to more greenhouse gases and cause global warming. Nuclear power, a recent source of energy, is harmful because of the dangerous radioactive waste it produces. Thus, there is now a search for alternative fuels. These include renewable sources of energy, such as the sun, the wind and even waves.

Alternative Energy to the Rescue?

Energy from alternative sources can be put to several uses. Solar energy can be used as a source of electricity, and heat. Wind energy can produce electricity, grind grain and run pumps to drain out water. Energy from waves can be used to generate electricity and pump water. Energy from biomass, which includes crop waste, grass and husks of grain, can be used in factories. Energy from biomass can even be used to light up homes and villages and for cooking.

Solar energy can be used to produce energy

Cleaner Fuel

Alternative fuels, such as solar, wave and wind energy, are renewable. Sources of fuel, such as biomass, are cheaper than petroleum and other fossil fuels. They are also safer than nuclear power. An accidental leak from a nuclear power station can cause a huge disaster. For instance, on 26 April, 1986, the Chernobyl nuclear power plant in the Ukraine, exploded and caused the death of 57 people. The ongoing impact of the radiation in the region is still being felt to this day and has caused the death of many more.

ECO fact

Oil constitutes about 40 per cent of the world's commercial energy. Transport, in the form of road, rail, air and water uses 60 per cent of the total oil produced.

Nuclear power plants are a contentious form of energy supply

23

Photovoltaic cells trap solar energy to be used for different purposes

Solar Energy

Without the sun there would be no life on earth. Solar power is an alternative source of energy that is being increasingly used in many parts of the world. It is a safe and clean source and there is no fear of it ever running out!

Shining Bright

Solar energy can be put to a number of uses. Energy from the sun can light up our homes, streets and offices. Several cities use solar energy to power traffic lights. For centuries, people in cold places have built their homes to face the sun. Modern technology can convert sunlight into electricity through photovoltaic cells or by heating a liquid that runs a generator through steam. It is used to heat water and warm rooms, and even to cook food by the same process as an electric oven. Solar energy can also be used in household activities, such as ironing.

Warming Up

Energy from the sun is used to heat spaces and to keep rooms ventilated. It is used in industries and to distil and disinfect water. Solar cookers are used for cooking food. It can even be used to pasteurise milk.

Revving Up With The Sun

Solar vehicles are powered by the sun's energy, which is trapped by panels on the cars. These photovoltaic, or PV, cells turn the sun's energy into electrical energy that powers the car. There are at least two car races only for vehicles that run on solar energy: the World Solar Challenge and the North American Solar Challenge, both held in America.

Several concept car are now being manufactured that use solar energy

Solar cookers convert Solar energy into heat, to cook food

ECO fact

Bysanivaripalle is the first village of its kind in India to use only solar cookers! Every home in the village has been cooking with solar since 2004.

Water Power

Hydropower is the force of water. It is one of the oldest sources of energy and has been used by people for centuries. It is free, safe and does not produce any waste.

There were 5,624 water mills south of the Trent River in England in 1086

In The Past

Hydropower is one of the largest renewable sources of energy. Water power has been used for many years to move wheels attached to a grinder to grind corn or flour. The wheels were often placed in the middle of the river, which turned with the flow of the river water. These were known as water mills.

Types Of Water Power

Tidal energy is a form of hydropower that uses tidal currents in water to generate energy. The water turns turbines that convert the energy into electricity. As two thirds of the world is covered with water, the potential energy of the sea is enormous. However, there are enormous costs and risks involved, as well as potential environmental impacts.

Light In Our Lives

One of the most important uses of hydropower is to produce electricity. In most countries, large dams are built across rivers to hold water. This water turns turbines, which convert the energy into electricity. Hydro-electric energy is cleaner and cheaper than energy produced by burning fossil fuels. However, the construction of large dams and power plants on rivers harms fish and other water creatures that live there. Dams often involve the displacement of large numbers of the population, as people are moved to make way for the large flooded areas that are to be created.

Tidal power stations convert tidal energy into electrical energy and other forms of energy

Large dams built across rivers harness the energy from the water. This energy is safe, clean and renewable, but does come with its own environmental impact

ECO fact

Hydropower is the world's largest source of renewable energy and constitutes about 7 per cent of the total energy worldwide.

Movement of Hot and Cold air

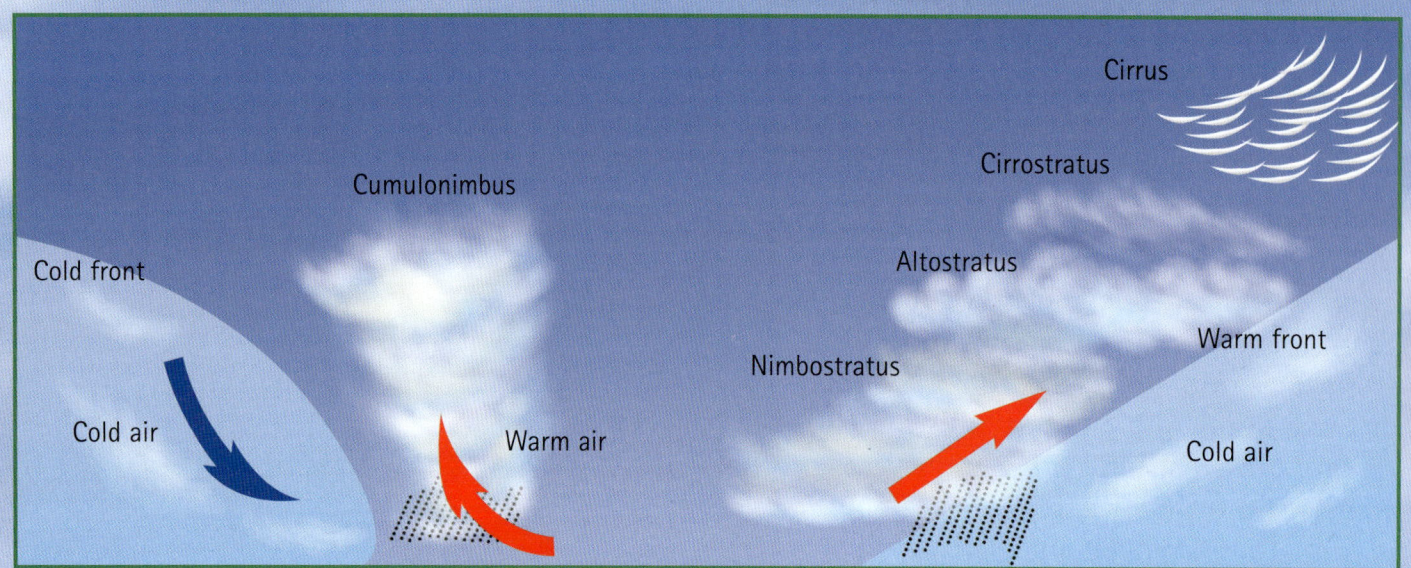

Cirrus

Cirrostratus

Cumulonimbus

Altostratus

Cold front

Warm front

Nimbostratus

Cold air

Warm air

Cold air

Wind Energy

For thousands of years, people have used the power of wind to their advantage. Wind power is the conversion of wind energy into other forms of energy, such as electricity.

Blow, Wind, Blow!

The wind blows because of the sun. Heat from the sun warms the air. Hot air rises and cool air rushes in to fill the space. Since the entire world cannot be heated evenly at the same time by the sun, the wind is always blowing. This wind energy can produce electricity, grind grain and run pumps.

ECO fact

According to scientists the best places in the world to generate wind power are in Northern Europe, the southern tip of South America, Tasmania and the Great Lakes region in the U.S.A.

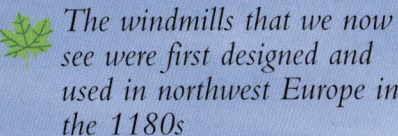

The windmills that we now see were first designed and used in northwest Europe in the 1180s

The Miller's Best Friend

Early windmills used wind energy to turn their sails. Windmills turn the wind's kinetic energy into mechanical energy. Modern wind turbines turn this kinetic energy into electrical energy. These modern windmills or wind turbines may not look much like the windmills that ground corn, but most of them still use two or three blades to catch the wind's energy.

One Windy Day

Wind blows throughout the day and night, but it has hardly been used to produce electricity in recent years. Countries have not used wind energy as much as they could. Just one per cent of the total electricity in the world comes from wind energy. Wind is a free source of energy, which is clean and does not cause pollution. However, no one has yet been able to predict how much wind will blow at a given time, and so, it is an uncertain source of energy.

Wind powered generators throughout the world produced 73.9 gigawatts of energy at the end of 2006

29

Bio Fuels

Bio fuels are made of anything that was once alive, or derived from biomass. They may also be made from products released by living creatures. Bio fuels, such as wood, are the earliest forms of fuel known to humans.

Back To Bio

People have been using bio fuels for thousands of years. They collected dry twigs and branches to cook their food. They made cow dung cakes out of bits of straw mixed with cow dung. The use of bio fuels decreased from the time of the Industrial Revolution. Most machines were run on fossil fuels, which are non-renewable. It was due to the rising level of pollution caused by fossil fuels that people realised the need for bio fuels.

Wood is still used in many parts of the world for cooking food

This innovative vehicle is run on hydrogen and vegetable oil!

From Anything That Lived

Bio fuels can be solid, liquid or gaseous. Stalks of crops that have been harvested can be used as fuel. Animal fat and oil from plants are also bio fuels. Even waste can be turned into fuel. Rubbish thrown in a landfill starts to decay and gives out landfill gases, such as methane. These bio gases can be burnt as fuel and used for generating electricity. Waste from animals and human beings can also be made into bio fuels. This is another form of bio gas and is used for lighting and even cooking.

Powered By Plants

Ethanol is made mostly from fermenting corn, yeast, sugar and water and is an alternative fuel. Bio diesel is also made from plants like soya beans and oil seeds, animal fats and vegetable oils. These fuels release carbon when they are burnt and are known as carbon neutral fuels. This is because the amount of carbon dioxide absorbed while it was alive is the same as the amount it gives off when burnt as fuel.

There are large bio gas plants which produce bio fuels to be used for various purposes

ECO fact

Ethanol is used in some parts of the world, such as Brazil, to run automobiles. These vehicles start on gasoline, but switch over to ethanol once the engine is running.

ROGEN & VEGGIE OIL POWERED

Hybrid Vehicles

A hybrid is a combination of two different things. A vehicle that can run on two or more different types of energy, is a hybrid vehicle.

Why are Hybrids Important?

Hybrid vehicles take the best advantage of different fuels. For instance, a hybrid electric car has the efficiency of an internal combustion gasoline engine and the electric motor that can save fuel and increase power. Some hybrid vehicles save gasoline by shutting off the engine when the vehicle stops.

What Lies Beneath

Ethanol, or grain alcohol, is made from corn, agricultural crops and agricultural waste, such as straw, and even from paper. Methanol or wood alcohol is made from wood, natural gas and, sometimes, from coal. Methanol powered cars are even raced.

Methanol powered cars are used in races like the Indianapolis 500

Hybrid vehicles are less noisy than single-energy vehicles

Large vehicles, such as trains, can also be hybrid. These trains run on electric and diesel engines

How Big Can Hybrids Get?

Any vehicle, from bicycle to train, can be hybrid. Buses, trucks and even ships can run on different kinds of energy. One of the major reasons every vehicle has not turned hybrid is because these dual system vehicles can be expensive. But not all cars need separate systems for two fuels, as gasoline can be mixed with ethanol, for example.

Recycling

Recycling is the process of re-using something after its first use is over. Recycled things are often used in a new way. If your shoelaces begin to fray, you can recycle them by tying them up in knots to make a key chain. Old things are recycled in factories to make something new.

Why Recycle

Many cities are running short of land for landfill. This means there is too much rubbish and too little space to keep it in. Rubbish rots and can smell. Landfills look ugly and can poison the land and water around them. When you recycle something you are easing the pressure on landfill. An added benefit is that the need for the mining for more aluminium for new cans is reduced; this saves time and energy and reduces the emissions of greenhouse gases.

The more we throw away the bigger our landfills grow

What can be recycled?

Recycling begins with separating things that can be recycled and then having them collected for recycling. Paper, plastic, metal, glass, rubber, as well as cardboard and cloth, can all be recycled. The recycled product can be the same as the original item, like an aluminium can, or it can be something very different. Even leftover food can be recycled. Rather than throwing it in the bin, kitchen waste like vegetable peel can be kept in a closed bin, mixed with soil and garden waste. In a matter of months, this mixture turns into compost, which is a type of fertiliser that helps plants to grow.

Compost provides important nutrients on which plants thrive

ECO fact

Currents in the Pacific Ocean have created an enormous area of human waste (mostly plastic) at sea that threatens wildlife. The phenomenon is known as the North Pacific Gyre.

Each Of Us Can Pitch In

Recycling is a way of managing and reducing waste. Waste management begins at the time we buy something. If we buy only what we need, then we have less to throw away. As a society we are very wasteful. Before you throw something in the bin, think if it can be used again, recycled or made into compost. In this way each one of us can help to reduce the amount of waste we produce everyday.

Recycling factories use waste products to manufacture new things

You Can Help

Reducing, reusing and recycling are three simple ways to reduce the amount of rubbish we produce. It's easy to do, it just takes a bit of thought!

The First 'R'

It is important to reduce the number of things we buy in order to reduce the amount of waste that we produce. Although we might think we need all the things we buy, we often end up with much more than we actually need. Before you go shopping, write a list of what you need to buy. Shoppers who care for the environment buy smart. They pick products that come with the least packaging. They buy just what they need, rather than being lured by bargain offers that lead them to overconsume.

Using cloth napkins instead of paper is a simple way of reducing waste

Reusing things helps to reduce waste. Pens with refills can be reused several times over

The Second 'R'

Reusing something means making its life longer, rather than throwing it out and buying something new. Use-and-throw products like pens and gas lighters, for instance, can be replaced by pens with refills that can be changed and lighters that can be refilled. In this way the amount we throw away can be reduced.

The Third 'R'

Even if we reduce the number of things we buy and reuse things, some things still need to be thrown away. This rubbish should be sorted out into two piles - things that can be recycled and things that cannot. Use two separate bins for this. Most plastic, metal and paper can be recycled. Aluminium foil packaging can usually be added to that. So can cardboard, including toilet paper tubes, egg cartons and paper boxes. A third bin should be kept for food waste that can be composted in your garden.

ECO fact

Each person in America wastes 74 kg of food per year. Britain dumps about 6.7 million tonnes of unused food every year.

Use bags made of recycled and recycleable material

Making Anew

Anything biodegradable can be broken down into raw form with the help of bacteria and other living organisms, such as worms.

Re-milled timber is often made into timber flooring and other products

Paper pulp is used to make new paper from used paper

Wood Forever

Small pieces of timber waste need not be thrown out. They can be recycled and made into useful things. Reusing wood from old furniture and old buildings is a simple way to fit the old into a new place. Wood that cannot be saved or has broken into small pieces is recycled by putting it through the mill again. Poor quality wood can be made into mulch and laid out over banks to stop soil from being washed away. If the wood cannot be used in any of these ways, it can be used as fuel in factories or in homes.

Pulp To Paper To Pulp

Over 40 per cent of the wood that is cut down is made into paper. It can be recycled and made into new things, including new paper. No piece of paper is too small to be recycled. The paper is first made into pulp by adding water. It is then beaten to separate fibres and then put through a screen to filter out larger pieces. The pulp is kneaded and bleached and made into paper. Recycling a tonne of paper saves at least that amount, or more, of wood.

ECO fact

The Ecopod is a coffin made by a manufacturer in the United Kingdom. It is made from paper pulp from recycled paper that hardens into a biodegradable box.

Earth To Earth

Biodegradable waste, including animal and human waste, can be composted. It is decomposed by bacteria and fungi and insects like ants and earthworms. Large amounts of biodegradable waste can be turned into biogas, which is a renewable source of energy.

Biodegradable waste can be composted at home in a compost bin or similar

Facts at a Glance

- The United Nations Environment Programme launched the Plant for the Planet: Billion Tree Campaign worldwide. The target for 2008 is a billion trees. Find out how to plant a tree at http://www.unep.org/billiontreecampaign/howtoplant/index.asp

- Many medicines are made from plants. However, less than 1 per cent of tropical trees have been tested by medical scientists.

- The Philippines has lost 97 per cent of its original forest cover and is home to some of the most critically endangered birds in the world.

- Malaysia has 681 threatened plant species, the most in the world. Many of these are timber trees. Indonesia follows with as many as 384 threatened plant species.

- Madagascar has the greatest number of critically endangered primates in the world.

The USA is rich in inland water species. It is home to over 60 per cent of the world's crayfish species. It also has the greatest diversity of salamanders and freshwater turtles in the world.

The rainforests are home to more than 900 threatened species of birds.

Over 14 per cent of the earth's land surface was once covered with rainforests. The coverage has drastically reduced over the years and rainforests now cover a mere 6 per cent. Some experts claim that the remaining rainforests could disappear in less than 40 years.

Loss of habitat is the single biggest threat to birds, animals and plants. Loss of habitat affects 89 per cent of all threatened birds, 83 per cent of threatened animals and 91 per cent of threatened plants.

Introducing alien plant and animal species can damage local plants and animals and in the worst instances lead to the extinction of the native species.

Young Activist

⊘ To save water:

- Watch out for dripping taps. One tap left dripping overnight can fill a bucket of water. That is 30 buckets a month!

- Generally, a shower will use less water than running a full bath (although some strong power showers can use almost as much). Consider showering instead of running a bath.

- If you are helping to wash up the dishes after a meal, use a washing-up bowl rather than continuously running the tap in order to save water.

Avoid running the tap continuously when you wash up

Let as much light in as possible during the day and turn the lights off to save electricity

⊘ To Save Electricity

- If you can switch the lights off in your room half an hour earlier every night, you save 15 hours of electricity in a month!

- Draw the curtains to get more natural light in your room and use less electricity.

- Switch off the television and computer at the wall. Keeping them on standby uses electricity.

- Turn off lights in rooms you are not using.

✔ To Reduce Plastic Waste

- Carry a reuseable bag whenever you go shopping.

- Make your own penholders and spoon holders from used plastic containers, rather than buying new containers.

- Cover books with brown paper that has no plastic coating. Better still, cover books with old calendars. The paper is strong and the pages are bright!

- Make your own gift paper out of old newspaper rather than buy plastic-coated sheets. Paint your own designs on them for that personal touch. Wrap smaller gifts in colourful cloth napkins.

 Beautiful and unique cloth bags can be made from old clothes and garments and used while shopping instead of plastic bags

✔ To Reduce Food Waste

- Take smaller helpings rather than one big helping that you may not be able to finish.

- If you are eating out, request the extra food to be packed for you to take home, rather than be thrown away.

Most restaurants will be happy to give you a doggy bag for any food you don't finish

Glossary

arsenic: an extremely poisonous metalloid that has many forms. It is usually yellow in colour and is commonly found in insecticides, pesticides and herbicides.

biomass: fuel derived from organic matter. This includes plant and animal matter and is used for producing heat, chemicals or fibres.

Bishnoi sect: sect originating in western Rajasthan in India. They believe that all living beings have the right to live and have gone to the extent of giving up their lives to save plants and animals.

compost: organic matter that has decayed.

ethanol: an alcohol derived from grain. It is colourless and often used in industry.

fossil fuel: fuels such as coal, petroleum and natural gases, which are formed from plants and animals over millions of years.

global warming: the heating up of the world as a result of man-made activities.

Industrial Revolution: a period of major changes in the fields of agriculture, manufacturing and transportation in the late 18th and early 19th centuries.

Kyoto Protocol: a meeting held on 11 December, 1997, in Japan. Steps to reduce the harmful effects of greenhouse gases were discussed.

methane: a colourless, odourless flammable gas that is the main constituent of natural gas.

methanol: a toxic, colourless, volatile flammable liquid alcohol, originally made by distillation from wood.

photovoltaic cells: cells that convert the sun's energy into electrical energy.

transpiration: the process by which water from plants is evaporated from those parts of the plant that are exposed to the air, such as leaves.

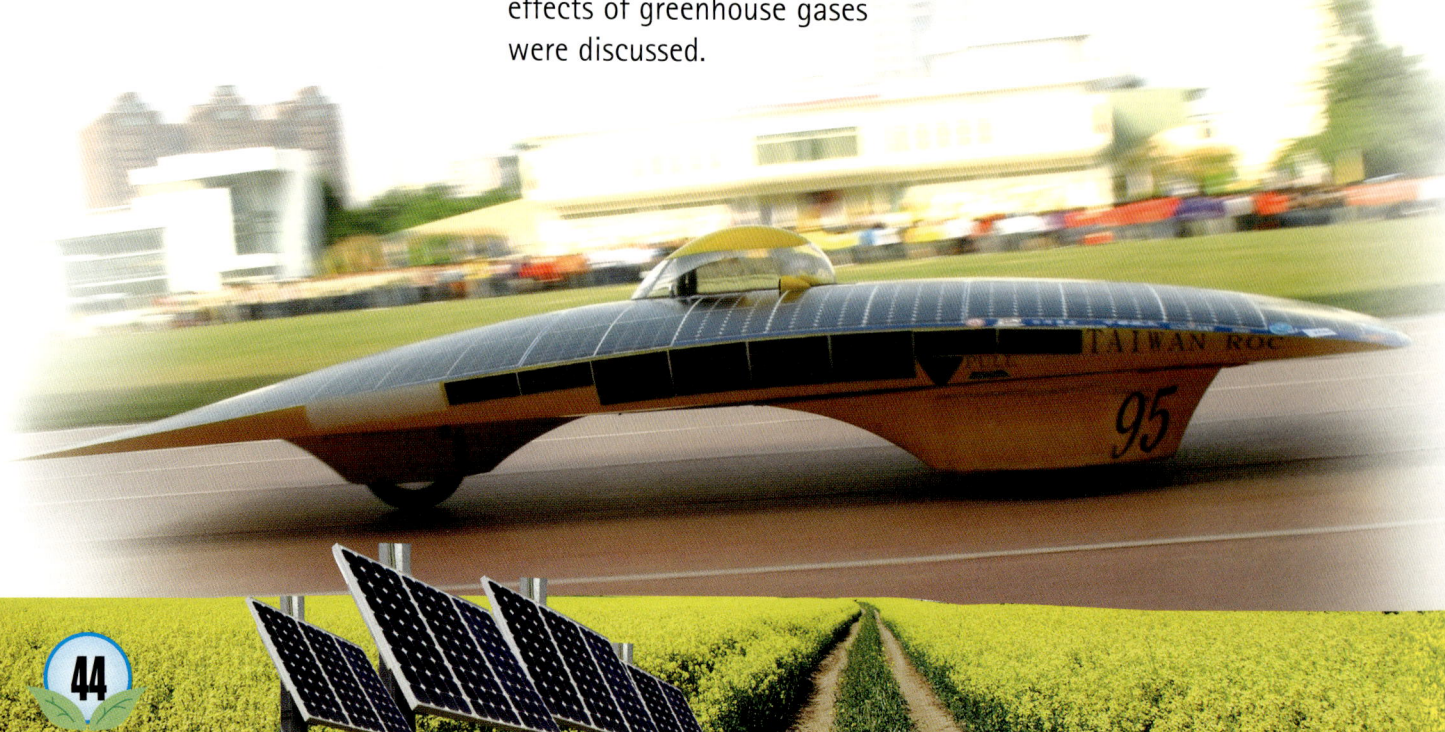

Index